EVEN BAD DOGS GO TO HEAVEN

MORE FROM THE DOG CHAPEL

STEPHEN HUNECK

Abrams, New York

Editor: Maggie Lehrman
Designer: Kara Strubel
Production Manager: Alison Gervais

Cataloging-in-Publication Data has been applied for and may be obtained from the Library of Congress.

ISBN 978-0-8109-9629-8

Printed and bound in China
10 9 8 7 6 5 4 3 2 1

Abrams books are available at special discounts when purchased in quantity for premiums and promotions as well as fundraising or educational use. Special editions can also be created to specification. For details, contact specialmarkets@abramsbooks.com, or the address below.

THE ART OF BOOKS SINCE 1949
115 West 18th Street
New York, NY 10011
www.abramsbooks.com

All dogs deserve a good home.

This book is dedicated to all the people who work tirelessly to try to make that not just a dream but a reality.

Sadly, Stephen Huneck, my husband, soulmate, and best friend, passed away shortly after completing this book. Stephen built the Dog Chapel and wrote the two *Dog Chapel* books to help people find closure after the devastating loss of a beloved dog. Equally important to helping people grieve was Stephen's commitment to helping people learn to experience love, joy, and laughter in the present by spending time with their dogs, especially when surrounded by nature's beauty. Stephen believed having several dog companions over a lifetime reminds us that "dying is a natural part of life."

At the end of *The Dog Chapel* Stephen writes, "You too can build a chapel in a place that is always open—in your heart." It is my hope you will hold Stephen warmly in your hearts. My heart is full of love for this gentle, generous, and, let's not forget, funny man.

Stephen, may you and all God's creatures find peace.

Your loving wife,
Gwendolyn Huneck

INTRODUCTION

It is hard to believe that it has been ten years since I finished building the Dog Chapel and almost that long since I first wrote about my mission in *The Dog Chapel: Welcome, All Creeds, All Breeds. No Dogmas Allowed.* Looking back on these years, I realize more and more that my life has been filled with miracles. Let me tell you about a few.

Fifteen years ago I became gravely ill. I was in a coma for two months. The doctors had little hope for my recovery, but recover I did. I had to learn to walk, write, and carve all over again. You've heard the expression, "What doesn't kill you makes you stronger." My illness did make me stronger, and it also made me more sensitive, and more appreciative of life. For most of my life before my illness, I had been a solitary person who spent his days working alone in a studio with dogs for company. I really didn't know very many people. That was destined to change.

Another expression you often hear is, "Love heals." I didn't understand the meaning of that phrase until I experienced firsthand the healing powers of love. I received extraordinary love from my wife, Gwen, while I was in a coma, but I also received unconditional love from complete strangers.

During my illness, news stories appeared about my being hospitalized and in a coma. When my wife was interviewed, she asked that everyone send me positive thoughts and prayers of healing. Groups came together all over Vermont to pray for my recovery. Get-well cards started pouring in—more than the hospital had ever received for a single patient. Soon there were shopping bags brimming with cards. I had never met the vast majority of these well-wishers, but they felt they knew me through my art. They felt a connection.

It wasn't until I was out of the coma and back home that I had a chance to read those cards. Tears poured down my face. I felt so grateful. The universe had given me a second chance and I wanted to make the most of it.

During the time following my recovery, I thought a lot about life and death. I pondered the rituals we perform when a person dies, such as throwing a handful of dirt on the lowered casket to symbolize that the person has passed on, which helps bring closure for the living. Since dogs are family members, too, I thought it would be wonderful if we could create a ritual space to help achieve closure and lessen the pain when we lose a beloved dog.

I remember a particular evening early in my recovery very clearly. I was using a walker because my muscles had atrophied, moving with difficulty from one room into another so I could speak with Gwen. As I placed the walker over the threshold of the room a thought flooded my head: *Build a dog chapel*. My first reaction was excitement. And then I started thinking, "Geez, with what I owe in medical bills I'd be lucky to build a little dog house."

But for months I couldn't get the idea of the Dog Chapel out of my mind. I wanted to build a chapel in the style of an 1820s Vermont church on Dog Mountain, our mountaintop farm. I wanted it to fit into the landscape, as if it had always been there.

Although I had no money, I didn't let that stop me. I put the word out to some people I knew who tear down antique buildings. I told them I was looking for stained-glass windows for my Dog Chapel.

One day when I was at our gallery in Vermont, I got a call from a fellow who had just torn down an old church in upstate New York. He was sure the windows would be perfect. I asked him how much the stained-glass windows would cost and he told me six thousand dollars. This was a lot more money than I could come up with, but I knew I had to go and take a look, and worry about that later.

There was an elderly couple in the gallery while I was on the phone, and they asked me what the conversation was all about.

I explained my vision of building a Dog Chapel. They did not say to me, "You're crazy," which was the typical response. Being dog lovers themselves, they thought my idea of a Dog Chapel made perfect sense. They said, "Listen, tell you what. You agree to make us a six-foot harvest table out of tiger maple and we'll give you the six thousand dollars right now, so you can go over and buy those stained-glass windows." Of course I told them we had a deal!

I went straight over to look at the windows and the fellow was right, they were perfect. I just had to add my dog motifs to their circular panels. With that purchase, the Dog Chapel started to seem like a reality. Three years and a lot of work later I completed the Dog Chapel. I spared no expense or labor to make it just as beautiful as I possibly could.

As soon as the Dog Chapel was open to the public, I invited everyone who came to visit to put up a photo of their departed dog and to write a few sentences about what their dog meant to them. I set aside a

wall in the foyer of the Dog Chapel, which I called the Remembrance
Wall, for this purpose. I had envisioned maybe someday having the
foyer filled top to bottom with dog pictures. I never anticipated the
whole building—every single space—covered with photos and words of
remembrance, as the chapel is today.

When you visit the Dog Chapel you are totally enveloped with messages of love. It is a very moving experience—sad certainly, but also uplifting—to see how much everyone cherishes his or her dog. Grieving for a lost dog is one aspect of the Dog Chapel, but equally important is celebrating the joy of living and the bond between dogs and their owners. I wanted people and dogs to have the most fun they possibly could. To this end, I have put in hiking trails, ponds for dogs to swim in, and an agility course for them to play on. In the winter folks come and snowshoe with their dogs, enjoying the pristine surroundings and spectacular views.

Twice a year we host Dog Parties: one in August and one in October. Hundreds of people with hundreds of dogs attend the festivities.

Because we have so many dogs all together at once, people often ask me if we ever have dogfights. The answer is no—never! We rarely even hear a bark. We ask everyone to take their dogs off their leashes so they are free to play, swim, greet one another, and of course, sit by the food tables and ask for food (which we provide in abundance with a BBQ for dogs and people). Everyone has a ball!

When you visit Dog Mountain you will most likely meet our three dogs, Salvador Doggie and Daisy, both black labs, and Molly, our golden retriever. People often remark how calm and well behaved they are and ask me how we trained them. I didn't train them. They trained me! They trained me to be my better self. The only method we use to influence our dogs' behavior is to say, "You are so good" over and over again. So, good they are. Occasionally one will get into some mischief, and it's usually Salvador Doggie helping himself to a bite to eat. But, really, how serious is that? Not very! Another expression that my illness helped me understand is "Don't sweat the small stuff"—and just about everything is small stuff.

Dogs are inherently good, kind, and social creatures. That is why I have titled this book "Even Bad Dogs Go to Heaven," because of course there really are *no* bad dogs. In this book I've chosen to celebrate the entire life cycle of our dogs, from puppy to wise old friend. I hope to capture the spirit of the miracles that helped me through my illness and allowed me to build the Dog Chapel. Dogs bring us closer to nature, and they help us live in the moment and feel unconditionally loved. They give us so much and ask for so little in return. Like the Dog Chapel itself, this book celebrates dogs, life, and love. I hope you enjoy it.

CHAPEL

WELCOME
ALL CREEDS
ALL BREEDS
NO DOGMAS
ALLOWED

DOGS COME IN ALL
SHAPES AND SIZES

BIG DOGS

LITTLE DOGS

LONG DOGS

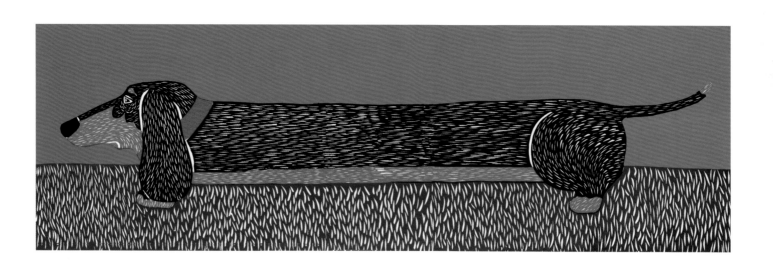

SHORT DOGS

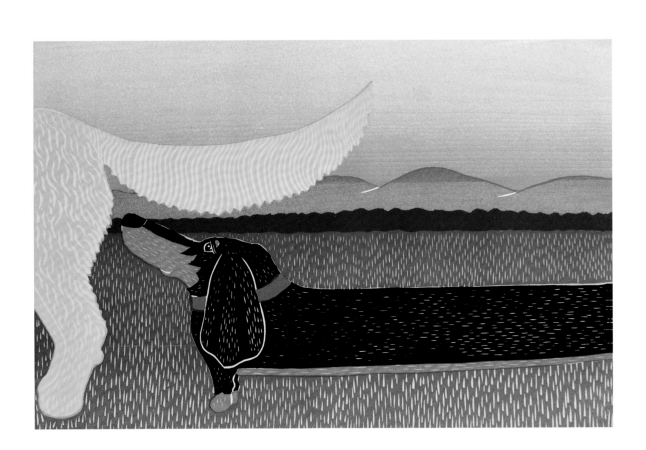

BUT A DOG IS A DOG
AND THEY ALL GET ALONG!

DOGS TEACH US
TO LIVE IN THE MOMENT

DOGS MAKE GREAT FRIENDS

WHEN YOU HAVE A DOG,
YOU WILL NEVER
EAT ALONE AGAIN

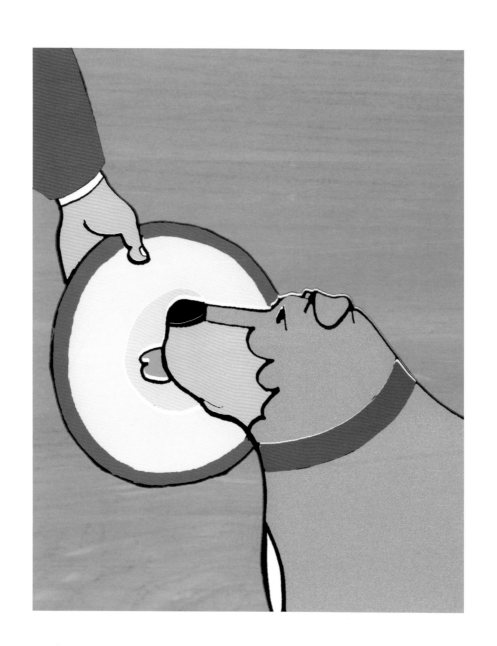

OR SLEEP ALONE

YOU WILL ALWAYS HAVE
A PARTNER

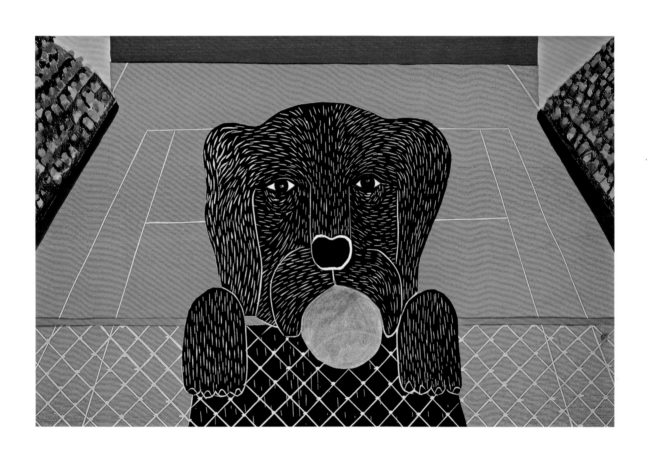

SADLY SOME DOGS ARE
BORN UNDER A BAD SIGN

BUT ALL DOGS DESERVE
A GOOD HOME

TREAT YOUR DOG AS
YOU WOULD LIKE TO BE TREATED

LOVE IS THE GOLDEN'S RULE

LOVE IS GIVE AND TAKE

THERE ARE THREE STAGES
OF A DOG'S LIFE

PUPPIES
(THEY ARE A HANDFUL)

ADULT DOGS

AND SENIOR DOGS

GOOD DOGS GO TO HEAVEN

BAD DOGS GO TO HEAVEN, TOO

EVERYONE MAKES MISTAKES

DON'T SWEAT THE SMALL STUFF

WATERBOWL

AND ALMOST EVERYTHING IS
SMALL STUFF

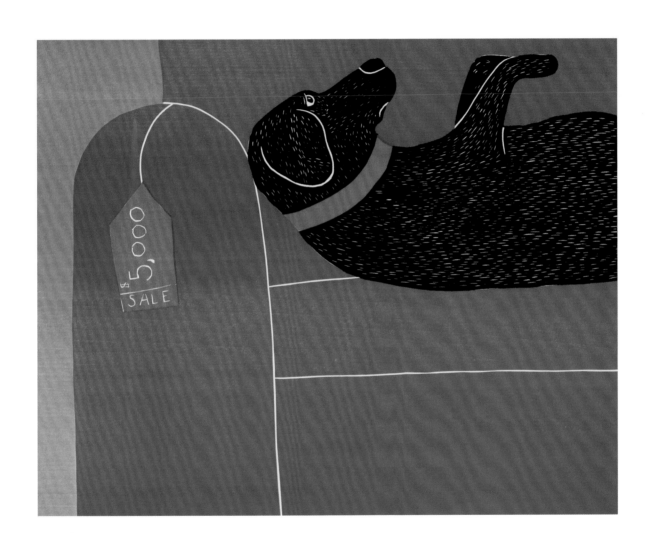

ALL GOD'S CREATURES
GO TO HEAVEN

DO DOGS DREAM OF HEAVEN?

OR DO DOGS DREAM
OF OTHER THINGS?

TREAT, GOOD DOG, SQUAB,
BRAUNSCHWEIGER, COOKIE,
CHICKEN DIVAN, SUKIYAKI,
HASENPFEFFER, GOULASH,
STEAK AU POIVRE, SIT,
COME.

LIFE IS A BALL,
SO LIVE IT TO THE FULLEST

WE WILL REMEMBER THEM
AND THEY WILL REMEMBER US

DOGS CAN SAVE US,
BODY AND SOUL

A LUCKY DOG!

DON'T BE AFRAID
TO LOVE AGAIN